Wooden Jewelry and Novelties

Mary Jo Izard

4880 Lower Valley Rd. Atglen, PA 19310 USA

Dedication

This book is dedicated to my daughter, Stephanie,
whose help proved immeasurable.
In fact, it couldn't have been done without her!

Copyright © 1998 by Mary Jo Izard
Library of Congress Catalog Card Number: 98-84398

Designed by Laurie A. Smucker
Typeset in Zurich BT / Zurich BLK BT

ISBN: 0-7643-0540-9
Printed in China
1 2 3 4

Published by Schiffer Publishing Ltd.
4880 Lower Valley Road
Atglen, PA 19310
Phone: (610) 593-1777; Fax: (610) 593-2002
E-mail: Schifferbk@aol.com
Please write for a free catalog.
This book may be purchased from the publisher.
Please include $3.95 for shipping.

In Europe, Schiffer books are distributed by
Bushwood Books
8 Marksbury Ave.
Kew Gardens
Surrey TW9 4JFEngland
Phone: 44 (0)181 392-8585; Fax: 44 (0)181 392-9876
E-mail: Bushwd@aol.com

Please try your bookstore first.

We are interested in hearing from authors
with book ideas on related subjects.

Contents

Introduction 6

Historical Background 9
  Where Did It Come From? 9

Wooden Jewelry 27
  Bracelets 27
  Pins 34
    People 34
    Plants 51
    Wildlife 61
    Western Wear 83
    Down Mexico Way 87
    Military Emblems 90
    Non-wooden Lapel Pins 95
  Necklaces 101

Wooden Novelties 106
  Address Markers 106
  Advertising Souvenirs 107
  Animal Figures 109

Bar-b-que Markers 110
Belts 111
Bookends 112
Buttons, Beads, Buckles & Charms 112
Christmas Ornaments 115
Dressing Items 116
Games 121
Key Chains & Key Racks 123
Kitchen Items 124
Masks 134
People 137
Pictures 149
Postcard Mailers 153
Toys 157
Weathervane 158
Whirligig 158

Bibliography 159

Acknowledgements

I wish to extend a personal "thank you" to all the people who encouraged me to put together the words and pictures that make up this book; specifically those of you who early-on saw the value of old carved wood and wanted others to do the same. My special thanks go to all those who allowed their wooden treasures to be photographed:

Lori Kizer, The Woodlands, Texas.
http://www.rhinestoneairplane.com or her E-mail at lorikizer@aol.com

Jimmy Jean Nuckles, Jimmy's Antiques, P. O. Box 96, Highway 29, Bertram, Texas 78605. Tel. 512-355-2985, or 512-756-2824. Jimmy's shop is treasure filled with artifacts, western memorabilia, cut glass, and primitives

Barbara Wood, Antique Pavilion, 2311 Westheimer. Houston, Texas 77098. Tel. 713-520-9755. http://www.BWoodAntique.com

Patti Howell, Tinhorn Traders, 1608 South Congress, Austin, Texas 78704. 512-444-3644

Andrew Church Antiques, Austin, Texas. 512-292-8445

Jim Charlile, A.B. McGill Antique Emporium, Highway 29, Bertram, Texas 78605

Jean Heath, Austin, Texas

Jean Bybee, Seabrook, Texas

Marilyn K. Bates, Houston, Texas

Arlene Cassens, Lampasas, Texas

Nancy E. Futch, Minden, Louisiana

Tim Pierson, Ardmore, Oklahoma

and those who wish to remain anonymous

Dealers represented in photographs from Uncommon Objects, 1512 South Congress in Austin, Texas, include Steve Wiman, D'Ette Cole, Ed Gage, William H. Baker, Gian Calaci, Joe Callison, Ned Coleman, Charity Cornelius, Gary Culpepper, Dot Dimiero/Dana Aichler, Susan Edwards, Jeff Garbs, Angelle Hall, Terry L. Hanson, Jean Heath, Joan and Jerry Maffei, M. Miller, Joel Mozersky, Joseph Nye, Charles B. Saenz, Staci Schwantz, Lucretia Sisk, and Steve Taylor and Evelyn Jones.

Shops represented at Uncommon Objects include A Woman With a Past, Andrew Church Antiques, Robert Barrett/Our Shop, and Past Times Antiques.

More thanks go to those who aided in the search for information: Catherine Yronwode, Forestville, California; Diane Bruce, Institute of Texan Cultures, San Antonio, Texas; Lucille Tempesta, VFCJNC, Glen Oaks, New York; Christi Romero, Sherman Oaks, California; Ginger Moro, Los Angeles, California; Kenneth Schneringer, Woodstock, Georgia; Jewelers Board of Trade, East Providence, Rhode Island; Sandy Groothoff, California Crafts, Anaheim, California; Greater Boston Chamber of Commerce, Boston, Massachusetts; Chicago Association of Commerce & Industry, Chicago, Illinois; Greater Philadelphia Chamber of Commerce, Philadelphia, Pennsylvania; Emily Clark, Chicago Historical Society, Chicago, Illinois; North & Judd, Middletown, Connecticut; Arlene Palmer, New Britain Public Library, New Britain, Connecticut; Chamber of Commerce; Albuquerque, New Mexico. These people were each very kind in attempting to aid the author.

Uncredited pictures are from the author's collection. Any errors within the text, picture credits, and descriptions are entirely the fault of the author.

Wood/honey Catalin 2" wide bead stretch bracelet. $45-65

Introduction

It looked so out of place ... this had to be the reason it came to be noticed. Strolling through an upscale antiques shop in a large retail shopping mall in northwest Austin, Texas, I came to a stop in front of an ornate display case. Nestled between a large display of exquisitely carved cameos on the left, and some delicate Nettie Rosenstein pins and earrings on the right, the jewelry I was taken by stuck out like a daisy in a bed of rosesFirst of all, it was wood. No big deal there. The cheapest medium available, right? Who'd want jewelry made from plain old wood? But still...

Upon examination, I was amazed. Not only was this 4.5" tall treasure made from wood, there were additional bonuses! My find was an Indian brave pin in dark brown carved wood who appeared to be doing a dance! His long black braid and feathered headband were painted and he wore leather nailhead-decorated leggings. Plus, he carried a green Lucite rattle!

It was love at first sight! Memories came flooding back of a childhood long ago in the small Texas border town of Del Rio. I thought of all the wood tourist pieces that were sold in the huge Mexican markets across the Rio Grande, and from vendors who wouldn't (or couldn't) pay rent for a market stall, but simply stopped shoppers on the streets of Villa Acuna (as the town was known then) hoping for a fast sale.

Suddenly, I remembered the inexpensive wood figural jewelry and local advertising items sold in the nickel & dime store in Del Rio (and in every small town across America). Toothpick and napkin holders, small wood carved 'valuables' boxes, salt/pepper sets, pencil holders, tacky poem plaques ... endless wood ... many pieces stamped with the hometown name and state, creating an instant souvenir.

But this dancing Indian brave was different ... beautifully made, with excellent detailing. After paying for this new treasure and tucking him into my purse, I pondered a search for another delightful piece like it. But where did the Indian brave come from, I wondered.

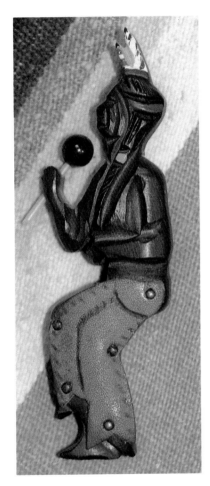

This little man started it all! Dark carved wood 4.5" Indian rain dancer pin, handpainted with nailhead studded leather leggins and a green Lucite rattle! $95-195

Years have now rolled by and I am still attempting to find the answer to my question. Other friends and antiques dealers have joined my fascination with wooden jewelry and novelties, and we have learned a lot. For those who seek such unusual treasures, a visit to the unique shop Uncommon Objects, in Austin, Texas, would be a treat. Uncommon Objects shines with a plethora of fabulous finds, especially those made from wood.

Current Values Range

Identifying a wooden product from something else isn't very difficult. But knowing the value of an item may be more difficult. The value and appeal in the marketplace depend on quality, design, workmanship, paint quality, desirability of subject matter, style and extent of carving, rarity, size, uniqueness, and condition. All these must be considered when purchasing wood pieces or other antiques.

But when a truly great piece is found with flaked paint or damage, the value should reflect its condition. Minor damage should not deter you from owning a great piece. If you are not buying it to resell, and it can add to your collection, there's something special about a minor blemish, like a baby's tooth marks from long ago.

In all types jewelry and collectibles, prices fluctuate in different markets across the United States. What sells well and for a certain price in Texas may go for nothing in Tennessee. What sells high in New York and California may go for much less in Kansas. The variation makes the business of antiques a great deal of fun.

And where do you find these treasures? At auctions, estate sales, antique malls, thrift shops, garage sales and flea markets. Finding really nice carved wooden pieces, either jewelry or collectibles, may take a little while. Develop an observant eye and keep up the search. Ask questions; tenacity will pay off.

How do you take care of wood jewelry and novelties? Whatever cleans and preserves natural wood, whatever prevents drying and deterioration of your wood treasure, should work. If paint is involved, be very gentle and use common sense in cleaning any wood piece. Read the directions fully on any cleaning compound container before using the contents.

The range of values mentioned in this book takes into account the variables concerning condition, and they are meant only as a place for you to begin. The lowest value, of course, is for a piece in only fair to good condition; the highest value is reserved for a piece in the finest condition. This author can take no responsibility for any reader's buying practices!

Buyers should always remember that nothing is worth anything unless you can get someone else to pay you for it. Keep this in mind when you buy.

Because of the wide range of styles, size, and condition of collectibles, the value ranges given refer only to those items specifically pictured within this book.

GOOD HUNTING!

Uncommon Objects in Austin, Texas

8

Historical Background

Where Did It Come From?

Where did a wood piece like the Indian brave pin come from? My search has lasted for years. I gradually came to realize that none of the wooden jewelry or novelties of this type are signed by a maker or marked by a manufacturer. Company after company that I contacted stated that they did not work with wood. Noone could be found to take credit for the whimsical, fanciful, endearing wooden pieces I was finding.

Dealers who had plastic and wood combination pieces always spoke as though the wood was not there; only the plastic was mentioned. Why? Both had been hand carved.

Perhaps heretofore working with wood was considered a "craft" ...not an "art." Perhaps carving a salt and pepper set from wood was thought of as a "hobby." Perhaps a carved and painted pin of a horse and rider was a "hobby craft." Webster's Dictionary definition of "art" and "craft" is not decisive here. Craft: "requiring skill." And hobby: "Something that a person likes to do or study."

More investigation and extensive careful reading brought some answers.

Hand Carved Jewelry

Carvers of plastics initially were wood carvers. This was made apparent in conversations with Rodrigo Moure, who owned Alta Novelty Company in New York City with his brother, Robert, between 1935 and 1940. Together they produced a large array of galilith and Catalin plastic buttons and jewelry, and some also incorporating wood. They used ebony, East Indian rosewood (pink hue), Brazilian rosewood (brown hue), and many Tibetan woods, of which there were many different and beautiful kinds. In some cases, the exotic woods cost the company more than the plastics.

Rod Moure was a specialized woodworker in his early years, even before going to work at age 19. Later, he worked for Gramercy Novelty Company, a manufacturer of plastic buttons, hair ornaments and pins. The Moure brothers have referred to Alta as their "Catalin and wood ornament business." This is quite revealing, and indicates that wood was an important element of that business.

Rod Moure did not sell Alta's products to certain stores which had their workers copy his designs. But Lord & Taylor in New York and Wanamaker's in Philadelphia were two of his favorite retailers. The people were nice and they sold Alta's products well.

One day a month Rod Moure , who designed all of Alta"s jewelry, would go to the New York Public Library at 42nd Street and 5th Avenue to study their exhibits for new design ideas. His favorites were Tibetan and oriental types. He also got new ideas from the movies and American life in general. Rod Moure produced the wooden jewelry and entire display for Tibet's exhibit at the 1939 New York World's Fair.

Many of the carved wooden pins in this study have an exact likeness to pins created in plastics. It is not known whether the wood pieces were prototypes for the plastics or vise-versa. Plastics and wooden jewelry designs were copied back and forth by companies who recognized a winning design and wasted no time in getting their own versions onto the market. It is assumed now that a great deal of the carved wooden jewelry presently on the market came from the same companies that hand carved plastics. Because the pieces are not marked by their makers, individual pieces are difficult to identify as being produced by a specific company.

On the east coast of the United States, the Alta Novelty Company in Manhattan and Ace Plastic Novelty Company in Brooklyn were known for their colorful carved designs in jewelry. On the west coast, California Craft Company, Authentics, Inc., Castlecliff Company, Coro, California Treasures, and Hobby House were known for their liberal use of wood in jewelry from the 1920s to 1945.

Top, a carved wood carousel horse pin with brass accents. $ 65-125 .Bottom, the same horse figure pin done in dark butterscotch Catalin with brass accents. $250-350

Left:
Look-a-like deer pins. Left, dark carved wood deer with leather ears. $65-125. Right, painted molded celluloid deer. $45-95

Left, butterscotch Catalin horsehead pin with glass eye, brass trim. $150-250. Right, the same pose in carved wood, glass eye, brass and plasteen trim. *Wood horsehead, Courtesy Lori Kizer.* $65-125

Smiling horsehead pins in wood and lucite. Top, carved painted wood with plasteen bridle. *Courtesy Marilyn K. Bates.* $65-125. Bottom, reverse-carved painted lucite. $85-145

February, 1931

No. 687. Delightful Mexican scenes to work in brilliantly colored strand cottons. And they'll do their part in adding charm and color to the home. The romantic balcony scene is for scarf ends; the flower vendor for a pillow. Running stitches, with outline and straight stitches give a woven effect. Two scarf ends, 12 x 18 ins.; pillow, 9 x 10. Yellow or blue transfer, 25c.

No. 688. More grand scenes from Western ranch life. The large scene (about 12 x 18 ins.) is for scarf ends, and the bucking bronco (about 8 x 9) is for a pillow top. Very exciting in bright strand cottons. The work is simply outline and darning stitch. For smooth linen, unbleached muslin or sateen. Two scarf ends and one pillow design. Yellow or blue transfer pattern, 25c.

From *McCall Needlework*, Winter 1939 Issue, this ad highlights the influence of colorful western and Mexican motifs in everyday life.

THE CALL OF THE WEST IN EMBROIDERY

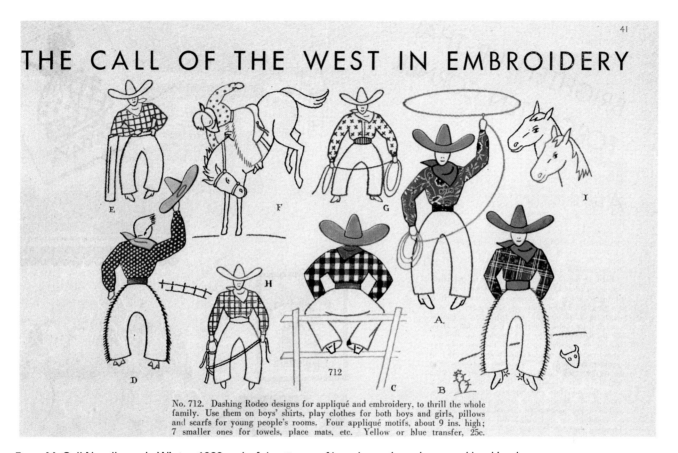

No. 712. Dashing Rodeo designs for appliqué and embroidery, to thrill the whole family. Use them on boys' shirts, play clothes for both boys and girls, pillows and scarfs for young people's rooms. Four appliqué motifs, about 9 ins. high; 7 smaller ones for towels, place mats, etc. Yellow or blue transfer, 25c.

From McCall Needlework, Winter, 1939, colorful patterns of bow legged cowboys and bucking broncos available for those skilled at embroidery.

Mexican Designs

Many of the painted wooden novelties represent images of rural Mexican life, including burros, cactus, men in sombreros, and dancing senoritas. Mexico undoubtedly produced a share of the carved wooden products. Many American homes today, after fifty or sixty years, retain these novelties, such as kitchen match holders which still rest atop the refrigerators.

Colorful Mexican clothing, such as gaily decorated, sequin covered, full skirts and puffy-sleeved, embroidered cotton blouses, were worn with waists encircled by hand-painted wooden disk belts that were joined together with brown rawhide strips or rayon braid.

Craft Kits

Home crafts kits were widely used from the 1930s through the 1950s. They were advertised in popular women's magazines, such as *McCall Needlework*, so that readers could order kits for wood crafts and jewelry to make at home. Companies such as Thayer & Chandler in Chicago, Shelart Studios in Florida, Kresge in Newark, New Jersey, Larch Book Company in New York ("Scrap Fun for Everyone" - 401 Things Anyone Can Make!), and Fireside Industries in Michigan all offered information and/or kits for home artisan work involving wood.

In January, 1942, *Comfort & Needlecraft Magazine*, published in Augusta, Maine, offered patterns and instructions for making a set of six wood figural plant holders, all for only 20 cents! In the winter of 1948, Walco Bead Company of New York City offered, for 25 cents, bead samples and a 32-page booklet entitled "Walco Wood Beadcraft Instruction Book."

An advertisement in the August 10, 1940, issue of *Saturday Evening Post* showed the United States Rubber Company using wood puppets to advertise their automobile tires.

Painted and carved wooden jewelry, and what we now call wooden novelties made during the period, were sold in the nickel & dime stores. Today, one has to wonder why these pieces were not signed? We can only surmise that the makers never thought that sixty years later someone would be asking this question. In fact, many of the other exquisitely made types of jewelry (and novelties as well) of that period also are not signed.

The Use of Wood in Jewelry and Novelties Before 1920

From the 1840s until the 1920s, jewelry and novelty manufacturing evolved quickly in variety and volume. Mass production enabled the cost of goods to come down so that nearly everyone could find goods to own. No longer was personal adornment reserved for the wealthy. Expensive, handmade jewelry encrusted with diamonds and set in high karat gold was imitated by means of a new process of electroplating and using non-precious stones such as topaz. The machine age in jewelry manufacturing had begun.

Among the jewelry imitations were those made from bog oak, a peat-bog wood from Ireland, and from gutta percha, a rubber material made from the sap of a tree. These can be considered examples of the use of wood in jewelry making during this period.

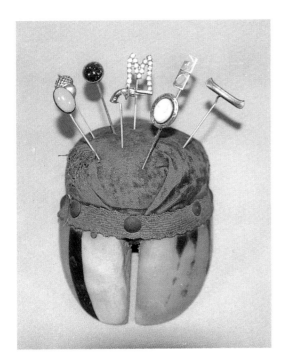

A Victorian cow hoof pin cushion, widely used in southern states during this period. Ultimately they fell from favor after being considered 'barbaric'. $45-125

Superior work. A tramp art box, date 1889 carved into front. Box done in carved stained wood with velvet trim. *Courtesy Andrew Church Antiques*. $200-300

Tramp Art

While the use of wood, other than bog oak, was not in favor for jewelry before about 1920, a whimsical wood craft known as "tramp art" was carried on from approximately 1880 to 1914, and has become a highly prized style in current markets. Itinerants, hobos (tramps), and prison inmates apparently did this intricate carving work using plentiful wooden cigar boxes. They turned out some rare treasures, including jewelry boxes, chains, comb & brush holders, doll furniture, picture frames and pencil cases. The makers cleverly made original designs using only a cigar box, sharp knife, glue, tiny nails and talent. These works of art now command high prices.

Beautiful color ad for wooden toys to be made at home from *The Designer Magazine*, December, 1917.

Old Friends in New Shapes
The Jolliest of Wooden Toys Readily Made at Home

Little robin wants to speak.
You'd think he could with such a beak!

CAPTAIN KIDD

Very stern and glum he glowers
But Baby plays with him for hours.

Simple Jocko wears a smile.
Play with him a little while!

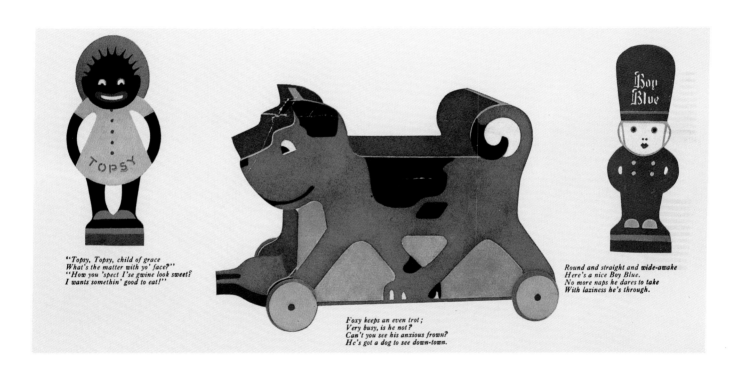

"Topsy, Topsy, child of grace
What's the matter with yo' face?"
"How you 'spect I'se gwine look sweet?
I wants somethin' good to eat!"

Foxy keeps an even trot;
Very busy, is he not?
Can't you see his anxious frown?
He's got a dog to see down-town.

Round and straight and wide-awake
Here's a nice Boy Blue.
No more naps he dares to take
With laziness he's through.

THESE stunning playthings, designed by Carter Housh, can be bought in the shops or made by a boy or girl skilled in the use of fret-saw and paint-brush. They are much larger than these pictures, but if the proportions are kept, can be made of almost any size.

I've had my Bob, my chicken toy,
Since I was just a little boy.
And I expect I'll like him when
I m running round with grown-up men.

Turk, my gobbler, plays with me
All day in my nursery.
Nights when I have had him fed
He sleeps with me upon my bed.

Many a fortune was foretold using the famous Ouija Board! This wooden piece was the one the fingers were placed upon, as the spirits guided it across the board and answered game players questions. Date of 1915 is clearly seen. $15-45

America Goes to War

When the First World War distracted many businesses from their production of consumer goods, people tended to make their own. Wooden crafts were popular even during these years, as evidenced by an ad from *The Designer Magazine* for December, 1917. "The Jolliest of Wooden Toys Readily Made at Home," this ad states, and shown are wooden pull toys of a bird, a monkey, a turkey, and a chicken along with a dog-shaped wagon to pull and toys in the likenesses of a toy soldier, Captain Kidd, and Topsy.

After the war, soldiers returned home and everyone wanted to celebrate in their own ways. Manufacturing expanded nationally and low-priced ornamental objects became available in quantity. And so... the 1920s were upon us and the jazz age was born.

The 1920s

During the 1920s, the quality of life for the average person improved over the relative austerity of the previous decade. Wood began to appear in popular jewelry designs in the 1920s, even though it had been used only sparingly during the previous century.

In the second half of this decade, Art Deco jewelry included styles made with chrome, steel, aluminum, bone, ivory, black onyx and obsidian, paste stones, turquoise, gilt, wire work, copper, marcasite, plastics and wood. Art

Deco designs included symbols of speed, electricity, transportation; impressionism, and cubism as well as geometrics such as squares, circles, triangles, and checkerboard patterns; flapper dancers and athletic figures; fast moving animals including borzois, greyhounds, antelopes, and fawns; Arabic and Oriental-inspired designs; and — with the 1922 opening of King Tut's tomb—Egyptian motifs abounded.

During this period were found necklaces of painted wood balls on cotton braid and large, hollow, glass beads dipped to look like pearls.

Barbaric Jewelry

In 1921 a new term was evolving in jewelry, "barbaric," but it took until almost the end of the decade before barbaric jewelry was accepted. The basic form of barbaric jewelry was big, chunky, and massive. It is a style of jewelry brought about by the liberal use of wood by 1928, along with other natural materials including shells, nuts, seeds, cork, felt, feathers, and leather. More than ten years later, these same materials, plus others, would again be introduced for use in jewelry making in the 1940s.

Companies producing popular jewelry styles, such as Castlecliff and Coro, offered jewelry lines of carved, gilded, painted, and feathered wood. The specific wood types included snakewood, rosewood, teak, ebony and African onyx.

Painted wooden beads in many bright colors were combined with bits of crystal, ivory, amber and glass, but the wood portion of the jewelry piece was meant to stand out. The unlikely combinations seemed to make this style even more popular!

Even some of the women's fashion couturiers of the period (Lucien LeLong, Norman Hartnell, Coco Chanel, Elsa Schiaparelli) offered jewelry styles made with wood, and usually the more massive the piece, the better!

Mexican Styles Emerge

In 1929, in the small Mexican town of Taxco, silver jewelry began to be produced under the direction of an American entrepreneur named William Spratling, an eventual leader in the local craft of jewelry making. Spratling had been a teacher of architecture at Tulane University in Louisiana when he vacationed in Mexico in 1925. Within four years he was living in Taxco and had hired a group of workers to learn the jewelry making business. Spratling's designs incorporated western and Mexican artistic motifs. He experimented with combinations of local materials and used some wood in his designs.

Financial Down-turn

The most memorable event of the 1920s, which influenced everyday life including that of jewelry adornments, actually had nothing to do with jewelry. On October 29, 1929, the economic failing of The New York Stock Exchange caused life to change for many people across the United States. Events conspired to cause the Great Depression to begin.

The 1930s

With the crash of the New York stock market in 1929, many people lost considerable wealth and the ensuing Depression cast a giant shadow over manners, attitudes, fashion, and adornments of the next few years. In the early part of 1930, fine jewelry was sold or hidden away in safety deposit boxes. The truly wealthy people, those unhurt by The Crash, still had their expensive baubles but they wisely chose not to flaunt them before the public. Many people's main problem was simply finding enough to eat each day.

When suffering abounds, humor helps; and so humor and the glamour of Hollywood's comedic movies of the 1930s offered weary

Shootin' up the town—that's what charming Sally Eilers gets away with in her newest talkie "Reducing." But she doesn't need to reduce. She has just borrowed her husband's (Hoot Gibson's) chaps.

This little doll has the 1930s look of a leading lady in a Hollywood western, with her painted wood face, leather hat, vest and tie, plastic rope, and real sheepskin chaps. $65-125

21

Depression-era citizens a heavenly escape from reality. The public idolized movie stars and imitated them in many ways. If people could not afford the fashions their idols were wearing on the movie screen, they probably could afford a new, inexpensive jewelry piece to update an old dress.

Therefore, it is not so surprising that the 1930s was a very healthy period for the inexpensive jewelry industry. New styles in great volume were able to be made and sold.

Fake was fine!

Inexpensive jewelry materials included glass beads, seed pearls, coral, garnets, lacey metal filigree, gold plate, white metal set with paste and rhinestones, large fake pearls in white and pastel colors, plus velvet ribbon (yes! ribbon), patent leather, nuts, felt, copper, fake gold coins, cork balls, and faux amber, turquoise, amethyst, ruby, and emerald, as well as many different plastics and that old standby, wood. Experimentation seemed to be the watchword during the 1930s, as the range of jewelry-making materials during the period proved so wide and varied that many times a single piece of jewelry was worked with a combination of two, three, or four different types of materials together, such as metal, plastic, felt, and wood.

Variety of Styles

Styles prevalent at the beginning of the decade included Victorian revivalist motifs including charm bracelets, cameos, chatelaines, dog collars, chokers, filigree pins of cupids, leaves and violets, lovebirds, ribbons furled and unfurled, lockets, charms and crosses. Later in the decade, heavy bib necklaces and chains with pendants, snake chains, and pairs of dress clips became very popular. But most importantly for this study was the "conversation jewelry" and the use of the new plastics that gained popularity in the middle of the decade.

Plastics from Wood

By 1935, colorful plastic jewelry was high fashion. Two common substances, wood and cotton, are actually the base raw materials from which many plastics occur. In both cellulose acetate plastics and phenolic plastics, the raw materials include wood or cotton lint. So, that beautiful piece of plastic jewelry owes its beginnings to wood.

Brightly colored plastics, some deeply carved, innovative, and wickedly witty, were hand painted and undercarved. The designs were ultimately worked with wood, Lucite, brass, leather, feathers and celluloid. Who then knew that the plastics craze, which began more than 60 years ago, would be with us still in the 1990s?

As the end of the decade loomed and Europe was entering World War II, imported raw materials dwindled in the United States. For jewelry and novelty manufacturing, the materials, design and production took a new turn. Enter wood ... on a grand scale. Not too costly, unique in its appearance yet able to resemble something else, easy to find and work with— wood was versatile. It laminated well to other materials, easily received paint, and was amendable to use with many other materials. What else could designers and manufacturers ask for?

The 1940s

On a recent trip to an area bookstore, it was astonishing to find over 60 books available to buyers covering wood and how to work with it. An unbelievable assortment offers woodcrafters information about turning wood into jewelry, walking sticks, furniture, animal figurals, kitchen utensils, gazebos, decks, and small whimsical items such as salt/pepper sets and napkin holders. These items also abounded in the 1940s as souvenir items. The Barbaric look of the early 1920s wooden jewelry styles, and the carved plastics and wood delights produced after 1935, anticipated the frequent use of wood for jewelry and novelties produced between 1940 and 1945. When the country's need to supply troops with goods during World War II brought about a shortage of jewelry-making materials in 1941, wood was already being used to give women fun and witty jewelry in designs with great imagination. During these war years, carved wooden jewelry was worn as a fun way to demonstrate patriotism. It projected the popular idea that, "I'm conserving for the war effort, but I still want to have a new piece of jewelry to adorn my overalls while I work at the factory for my country!"

The popularity during the 1940s of Western movies is illustrated by the extensive use of horses, cowboys, Indians, and Mexicans in the carved wooden jewelry designs of the era. This theme is carried out repeatedly, and although the really beautifully carved wooden figural pins are found only with a lot of searching (this from personal experience), the majority of what is found is thematic.

Delightful painted wood World War II military man jointed figure. *Courtesy Jean Heath*. $65-125

Whimsical souvenir novelties as well as potholder and necktie storage racks, picture frames, and cigarette dispensers display the same Western influences and Mexican painted figures. Full-skirted dancers, sombreros and serape-clad men, donkeys, stagecoaches, bucking broncs, cactus and desert scenes, guitars and dancing shoes all appeared throughout the decade.

During the 1940s these styles of novelty jewelry included not only the carved wooden pieces, but also painted ceramic clay and plaster, shell, nut and seed items, crocheted, felt and pipe cleaner pins which were homemade from kits. Craft magazines offered kits and instructions, using materials that were inexpensive and easily found. Ladies only had to look in their kitchen and sewing cabinets for rice, beans, pumpkin seeds and nuts, felt and bottle corks for decorations.

In the Summer, 1945, issue of *McCall Needlework*, there appeared a short article telling the reader, "A ball of crochet cotton, a crochet hook, some pieces of wire, and a pair of earring clips are all you need to make this rose spray and earrings set." Appropriate pictures accompanied the article.

An advertisement in *McCall Needlework* dated Winter, 1948-49, from Beaver Crafts. Inc. in Chicago, Illinois, stated, "You can create beautiful handmade jewelry" and offered a big handicraft book for only 10 cents. Copper, sequins, and shells are just some of the proposed ornaments presented by this book that showed projects using leather, plastics, and wood.

After the war was over, the popularity of art forms using wood in jewelry and novelties suddenly dropped. Sentimental and patriotic images were out of favor and it was time for new ideas.

Made in Holland

Jigsaw puzzle

Legpuzzle

Puzzle

Zusammensetzspiel

Rompecabezas

Quebra-cabeça

Puslespil

Puslespill

Paper envelope held color cardboard puzzle. Probably a giveaway to young passengers flying on KLM Royal Dutch Airlines. 1950s. $15-30

KLM Royal Dutch Airline color puzzle. Holland's idea of a Mexican scene using wood figures!

By 1947, this type of intricate crystal bib necklace had replaced wood in many of America's jewelry-loving hearts. Goldtone metal with shades of blue crystal and glass beads, this beautiful piece is unsigned. Late 1940s. $200-300

Dark stained carved wood Liberty Bell bar pin with brass trim. $35-55

26

Wooden Jewelry

Bracelets

Bangles. First three, left to right, plastic/wood. $20-65. Two on right, Catalin/wood. $35-75

Bangles. First three, left to right, plastic/wood. $35-75. On right, carved Catalin/wood. $95-195

From left to right, hinged carved wood/red Catalin. Hinged carved wood/Catalin flower top and red/black Catalin stripe with wood bangle. *2, 3 Courtesy Lori Kizer.* $125-225

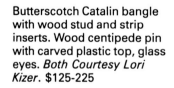

Butterscotch Catalin bangle with wood stud and strip inserts. Wood centipede pin with carved plastic top, glass eyes. *Both Courtesy Lori Kizer*. $125-225

Right:
Wood/Catalin hinged bracelet with turtle. Matching pin, brass eyes. $200-300

Above:
Carved wood dog pin with red Catalin swivel head, glass eyes. *Courtesy Lori Kizer*. $150-250

Carved wood and Catalin set. Pin, pair clips, hinged bracelet (with date 12-25-36 etched inside). *Courtesy Lori Kizer*. $250-350

29

Left:
Dark wood hinged bracelet.
Painted carved wood horsehead
over leather attached by laced
plasteen, painted eye. $125-225.

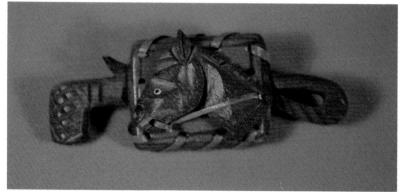

Pin matching the horsehead bracelet in lighter wood.
Horsehead, riding crop with plasteen and leather. $95-165

Detail of hinged bracelet top of horsehead over leather.

A saucy carved wood horsehead hinged bracelet. Glass eye, plasteen halter. *Courtesy Barbara Wood*. $125-225

Black painted wood hinged bracelet, brass initials inset on top. 1940s. $35-65

Carved wood hinged greyhound bracelet. Glass eye, painted tongue, collar. *Courtesy Nancy E. Futch*. $125-225

31

Carved wood/butterscotch Catalin hinged bracelet. Matching pin, plasteen knotted centers. $250-350

Carved wood / red Catalin hinged bracelet. $200-300

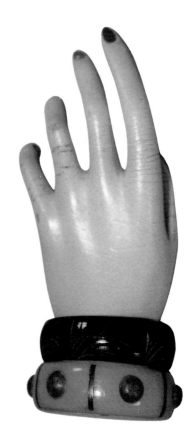

Bracelet. Painted wood bowling pins on brass chain link, matching clip earrings. *Courtesy Lori Kizer*. $45-85

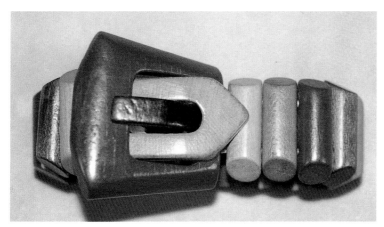

Colorful Czech painted carved wood bead stretch bracelet with working carved wood buckle. Two views shown. *Courtesy Lori Kizer*. $55-95

People, Faces

Painted black carved composition wood Aztec face pin, rhinestone trim. *Courtesy Patti Howell/Tinhorn Traders*. $65-95

Painted black carved polished wood girl's face pin, rhinestone trim. *Courtesy Lori Kizer*. $65-125

Hawaiian girl pin with winking eye and black hair. Wood with painted details. $35-55

Closeup of Carmen's hat crown filled with wood beads, leather leaves. Hat 4" across.

Carmen Miranda pin. A popular Brazilian singer/dancer from the 1930-40s. Many types jewelry and collectibles with her likeness can be found. $200-300

Closeup face view of the 4" painted carved wood face pin with colorful straw hat, purple celluloid earrings.

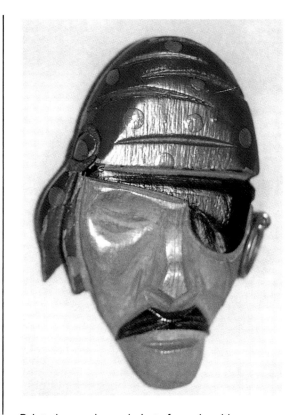

Painted carved wood pirate face pin with brass earring. *Courtesy Lori Kizer*. $95-145

35

Painted carved wood Apache dancer face pin with plastic cigarette. *Courtesy Lori Kizer*. $95-145

Old man face pin. Painted carved wood, Catalin eyes. *Courtesy Lori Kizer*. $95-145

Carved wood/cream galalith laminate Eskimo face pin. *Courtesy Lori Kizer*. $95-145

'Zoot suit' man face pin. Painted carved wood, open mouth, googly eye. $145-195

Another oriental painted carved wood figure pin with very short legs. $25-45

Oriental influenced painted carved wood face pin with very chubby cheeks. $25-452.75

Cowboys

Painted carved wood pin. Three circles with suspended horsehead and cowboy head, brass trim. $125-225

Painted wood rider on bucking horse pin, rather primitively carved. Plastic bridle. $45-65

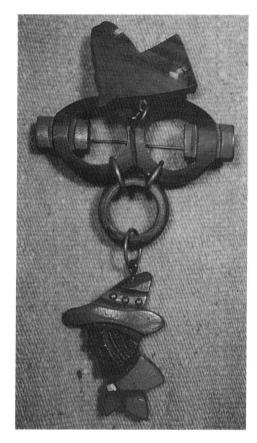

Intricate underwork is apparent in this view.

Carved wood cowboy face pin with painted applejuice Catalin face. *Courtesy Lori Kizer.* $150-250

Matching cowgirl face pin in carved wood/painted applejuice Catalin. *Courtesy Lori Kizer.* $150-250

Small pop-eyed cowboy face pin of painted carved wood, plastic hat brim and eyes. $35-65

Painted carved wood cowboy face pin with leather bow tie. $75-125

1936 Texas Centennial cowgirl pin. Painted details, machine stamped wood. $25-45

Jointed painted carved wood cowpoke pin, 5" tall. Plastic hat brim and pop-eyes, felt neckerchief. $95-195

Bow legged cowboy pin. Painted carved wood, very large red Catalin eye. *Courtesy Lori Kizer*. $95-145

Indians

Painted carved wood totem pole pin. $95-195

Three little Indians on arrow bar pin. Painted
carved wood. $35-65

Indian chief in top hat pin, feathers. Painted
carved wood. $95-195

Heap big Injun chief pin.
Painted carved wood, red
feather, brass earring. $75-150

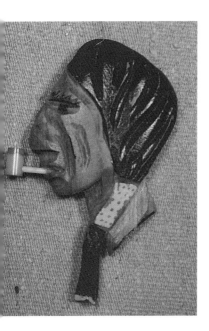

Indian smoking pipe pin.
Painted carved wood,
plastic pipe. $95-195

Ornate Indian chief pin. Horsehair braid, cotton/felt
headdress, plasteen ties, brass earring.
Courtesy Lori Kizer. $150-250

Black Americana

Unusual Minstrel Man pin. Painted carved
wood, leather top hat and bow tie, lucite
collar. $150-250

43

Lil' Smoker! Painted carved wood native face pin with butterscotch and green plastic, Catalin, brass, jute, and celluloid trim. $300-400

Ubangi native head pin. Painted carved wood, lucite headpiece, cotton fringe at neck. $95-145

Dark carved wood Ubangi pin. Elongated neck with brass, plasteen head wrap, brass earrings with red Catalin drops. *Courtesy Lori Kizer.* $95-145

44

Left:
Two carved wood native head pins. Left, painted. $45-65. Right, plastic hat and plastic/brass beads neckpiece. $75-95

Carved wood native head pin. Plasteen necklace, brass earring, plastic feathers. $95-125

Colorful painted carved wood Ubangi pin. Wood nose bone, celluloid earring, raffia hair, cotton yarn trim. $100-150

45

Right:
Elongated native face pin of dark carved wood with brass trim. $75-100

Another native head pin of carved wood. Jute, plastic, brass, and celluloid trim. $100-200

Carved wood native head pin. Plastic fruit headpiece/headwrap, brass earrings. $100-150

Left:
Colorful native head pin. Dark carved wood, red raffia topknot, plastic/brass headwrap, celluloid trim. $100-200

Right:
Pair native head pins. Left, painted carved wood. $45-65. Right, painted carved wood with jute, celluloid earrings. $95-145

Open-mouth native head pin in lighter carved wood with brass bell earrings. $75-125

Severe native head pin of dark carved wood with plastic, brass trim. $100-200

47

Special Characters

State souvenir glass from Alabama clearly showing a female Negro figure picking cotton. Probably early 1950s. Later glasses eliminated this scene. It then read simply ... Alabama The Cotton State. $20-40

Dutch boy carrying buckets pin. Painted carved wood, plasteen trim. $65-95

Painted carved wood tennis player figure within black Catalin frame, brass trim. $95-145

Googly-eye scarecrow pin. Brightly painted carved wood, plastic nose. $145-195

Painted machine stamped wood figure. Topsy?
$20-40

Snake charmer pin. Painted carved wood, lucite trumpet and snake, painted details. *Courtesy Lori Kizer*.
$125-195

Carved wood bellboy pin with keys. Brass trim. *Courtesy Lori Kizer*. $65-95

Very strange 6" bar pin? Three plastic figures balanced by painted wood strips. $15-30

Plants, Flowers and Gardening

A carved wood flower centers a carved lucite leaf pin. $35-55

Carved butterscotch flower pin on bed of carved wood leaves. *Courtesy Lori Kizer.* $75-125

Red Catalin poinsettia flower on carved wood base, brass trim. Perhaps a Christmas pin? $95-145

Carved wood/Catalin laminate pin, knotted plasteen center. $75-125

Watering can pin. Painted carved wood, painted carved Catalin flower shaped front, brass and string trim. *Courtesy Lori Kizer.* $100-200

Fan shaped Czech wood flowers pin covered with tiny machine-stamped painted flowers and beads. $65-95

Plain carved wood leaf pin with three bell type flowers. $35-55

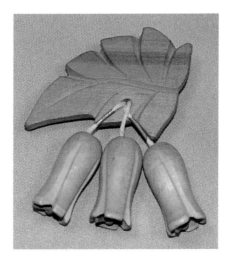

Exceptional carved wood flower pin with red Catalin stem and leaves. $125-225

Carved wood/painted plastic saw pin. *Courtesy Barbara Wood*.
$100-200

Left:
Carved wood flower with leaf and stem pin resting on 1940s hand-painted rayon tie. Pin $35-55. Tie $5-15

Shovel pin. Carved painted wood handle and applejuice Catalin shovel tip. *Courtesy Lori Kizer*. $100-200

Carved wood flower basket pin. Painted leaves, plastic flowers. $20-40

Three carved wood and Catalin pins. *All Courtesy Lori Kizer*. $95-145

Simple carved wood limb pin with white plastic flowers. $5-15

A wood/lucite turtle seems to study a carved wood stem pin with deeply carved red atalin flower. *Courtesy Lori Kizer*. Turtle $35-55, Flower $75-125

Fruit and Nuts

Red cherries pin. Carved wood leaf with painted wood cherries. $65-95

Carved wood log pin with red plastic berries. Restrung. $65-95

Right:
Very pretty painted red Catalin apple pin with painted carved wood base, added wood stem. *Courtesy Lori Kizer*. $175-250

Red painted carved wood cherries on carved wood leaf. Restrung. $95-145

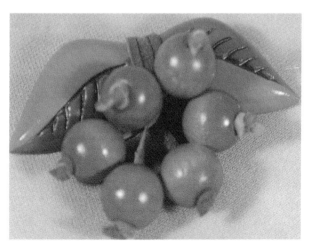

Painted carved wood oranges & leaf pin with rawhide trim. *Courtesy Lori Kizer*. $55-75

Pineapple pin in painted carved wood decorated with feather leaves. $45-65

Pineapple bar pin. Stained carved wood leaf. Pineapples attached by brass chain. $25-45

Carved lucite apple pin with carved wood stem. $75-125

Resin-washed Catalin leaf pin with attached carved wood acorns. Restrung. $150-200

Carved wood bar pin with carved wood leaves, circles, and real nuts. $65-96

Pecan head pin. Painted face, yarn/fabric headcover, celluloid earrings. *Courtesy Barbara Wood*. $15-30

Right:
Carved root beer Catalin leaf pin with carved wood acorn center. *Courtesy Lori Kizer*. $175-250

Carved wood pin with center of wood and brass beads, nuts, celluloid leaves. $10-20

Wood beads pin dotted with tiny beads, celluloid leaves. $35-55

Large and lovely wood beads pin. Colorful painted metal shank buttons give the look of a well-known chocolate coated candy. Wood leaves, plasteen trim. *Courtesy Marilyn K. Bates*. $55-75

Wildlife
Rabbits, Birds and Other Animals

Carved wood log pin with red Catalin bunnies, glass eyes. *Courtesy Lori Kizer*. $200-300

Fanciful painted carved wood rabbit pin, head swivels. $95-195

Carved cedar wood Texas jack-rabbit pin, painted details. $5-15

Painted carved wood owl pin, googly-eye, trembler hat. $65-95

Carved wood owl (head) pin, carved lucite (body and limb), painted details. *Courtesy Lori Kizer.* $150-250

Left:
Carved wood/root beer Catalin laminate bird pin with rhinestone eye. *Courtesy Lori Kizer*. $175-275

Carved wood/Lucite bird pin with painted eye. (Note chipped tail feather). $45-95

Flying duck pin. Dark green Catalin wings on painted carved wood. *Courtesy Lori Kizer*. $150-250

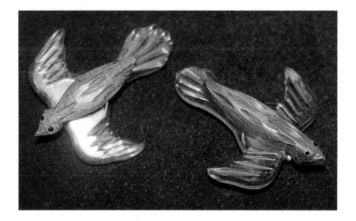

Pair painted carved wood/lucite bird pins. *Courtesy Lori Kizer.* $45-65

Carved wood bar pin with celluloid flower drop and chain holding painted red Catalin bird. *Courtesy Lori Kizer.* $65-125

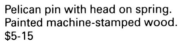

Pelican pin with head on spring. Painted machine-stamped wood. $5-15

Large carved wood/lucite swan pin. Brass eye and studs. $65-95

Flamingo pin. Painted carved wood with painted eye. $25-45

Whimsical carved wood ostrich pin.
Painted details, plastic tail, beak.
$125-195

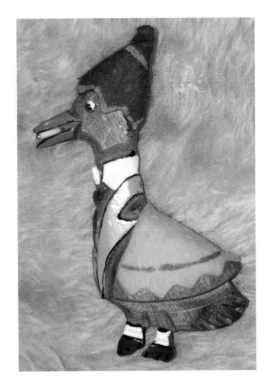

Smoking duck pin. Painted carved wood
body, plastic cigarette, felt coat, hat. *Courtesy Jean Heath*. $150-250

Painted carved wood dressed
human figure pin with dog's
face smoking plastic cigarette. $95-195

Camel pin. Carved wood/green Catalin laminate. $65-95

Back view of camel pin.

Left:
A very military Scottie dog pin. Painted carved wood, yarn on top hat, clutching brass sword. *Courtesy Barbara Wood*. $125-175

Cats and Dogs

Taking no prisoners, a painted carved wood cat invades reverse-carved painted Catalin fish bowl. Delightful pin. *Courtesy Lori Kizer.* $250-350

Strange painted carved wood pin of cat walking upright. $20-40

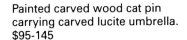

Painted carved wood cat pin carrying carved lucite umbrella. $95-145

Carved wood Scottie bar pin. Leatherette trim, glass eye. $35-55

Carved wood circle dog pin with painted details. $25-45

Wood dog pin. Yarn tail, ears, machine-stamped wood. *Courtesy Lori Kizer*. $15-30

Left:
Very odd pair of dogs pin. Painted carved wood with red Catalin center bar, one swiveling arm. $25-45

Weenie dog pin. Painted carved wood, plastic eye. $15-30

Carved wood Scottie pin. Glass eye, painted collar. $15-30

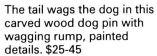
The tail wags the dog in this carved wood dog pin with wagging rump, painted details. $25-45

Bulldog pin. Painted carved wood, brass chain, red plastic lock. *Courtesy Lori Kizer*. $95-145

Dog face pin. Carved wood with plastic eyes, felt hat and tie. $65-12

Carved wood head of Doberman pin. Leather collar, painted details. $45-65

Amber rhinestone eyes grace a painted carved wood dog pin with silk necktie. $45-65

Carved wood dog head pin. Open mouth, glass eye, leather tongue/collar, brass studs. $65-95

Another pair of machine stamped wood dog pins with painted details. $15-30

Saucy painted machine stamped wood dog pin with bright red painted bow. $15-30

Pair of dogs. Machine stamped wood, glass eyes, painted details. $15-30

Cows and Horses

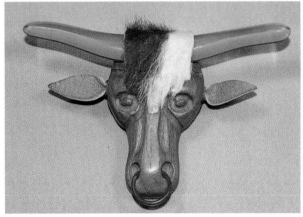

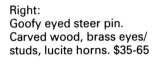

Right:
Goofy eyed steer pin.
Carved wood, brass eyes/
studs, lucite horns. $35-65

Texas longhorn pin. Carved wood, furry forelock,
leather ears, green Lucite horns, celluloid nose ring.
Horns measure 4.75" across. $195-295

Cow head bar pin. Painted carved wood, Catalin
horns, tiny velvet flower trim. *Courtesy Lori Kizer*.
$150-250

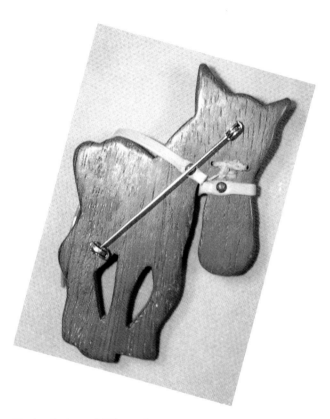

Little mule. Painted carved wood/orange Catalin laminate pin. Celluloid eyes, plastic reins, knotted plasteen tail attached with brass stud. $195-295

Pin back view of little mule.

Left:
Two donkey pins. Both carved wood, one with felt trim (and horns?), one painted. $25-45

Attentive donkey pin. Head on spring, painted machine-stamped wood. $5-15

Carved wood horsehead pin with three boot charms on brass. This same pin was done in Catalin. *Courtesy Barbara Wood.* $95-145

Carved wood pony pin. Lucite tail, mane. $20-40

Right:
Carved wood horsehead pin set in oval applejuice Catalin circle. Leather collar, brass studs. $125-225

Group of carved wood/lucite horsehead pins. Glass eyes, some painted details. $65-125

Bowlegged cowboys everywhere! Machine stamped painted wood cowboy pin resembles many of the western embroidery patterns that were favorites of needle-working homemakers of the time. (see page 13). $35-65

Painted carved wood horsehead pin. Plastic bridle, painted plastic eyes. $65-125

Carved wood whimsical pony pin. Brass saddle. *Courtesy Lori Kizer.* $45-65

Carved cedar wood horsehead pin. $15-30

Very detailed painted carved wood bucking bronc pin. Leather/plasteen trim, glass eye. $125-225

Carved wood bucking horse pin. Black paint highlights, plastic saddle, brass trim. $95-195

Painted carved wood horsehead pin with colorful twisted plastic mane. $35-55

Carved wood double horseheads pin with brass eyes. $25-45

Water Creatures

Clockwise, plain two color wood bangle. $5-10. Carved wood seahorse pin, snakeskin trim, brass eye. $45-65. Wood/Catalin turtle pin. $65-95

Right:
Carved wood/olive Catalin fish pin. $125-195

Carved wood seal pin balancing applejuice Catalin ball. *Courtesy Lori Kizer*. $95-145

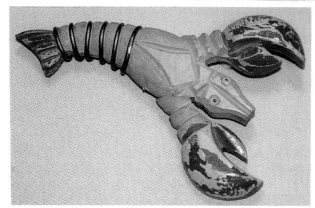

Carved and painted wood/lucite turtle pin. *Courtesy Lori Kizer*. $35-55

Painted carved wood lobster pin with brass trim (note flaked paint). $35-65

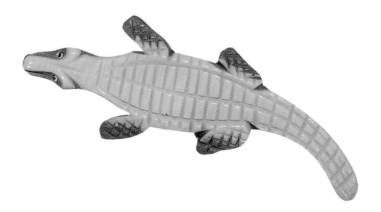

Carved wood alligator pin, pale green carved Catalin laminate top. *Courtesy Lori Kizer*. $195-295

Painted carved wood googly-eye fish pin. $35-65

Painted carved wood/lucite fish pin. $65-95

Unique carved wood/chocolate and olive color Catalin laminate frog riding alligator pin, glass eyes. *Courtesy Lori Kizer. $400-800*

Back view frog riding alligator pin.

Western Wear, Western and Bronc Busters

Carved wood horseshoe pin. Pair boots attached with plasteen. *Courtesy Lori Kizer.* $35-65

Carved wood horseshoe pin with brass studs.
$15-30

Right:
Well done cowboy on
bucking bronc pin, 4.5".
Painted carved wood. $195-
295

Very detailed man sitting on fence with grazing
horse pin. Painted carved wood. $125-225

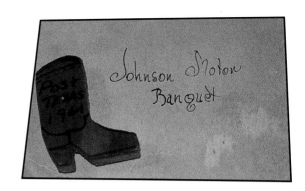

Right:
1941 place card. Johnson Motor Banquet, Post, Texas, carved wood boot attached. $10-20

Catalin saddle pin with four Catalin charms, centered with carved wood horsehead charm with glass eye. *Courtesy Lori Kizer*. $250-350

Cowboy hat pin. Carved wood, reverse-carved Catalin crown, plastic ball on hat string. $125-225

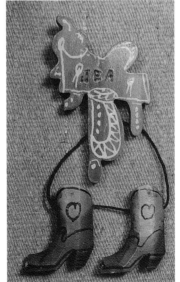

Saddle pin with boot charms. Machine stamped wood. Note initials scratched on saddle. $15-30

Wagons

Painted carved wood wagon pin. Reverse-carved Catalin (canvas) front with green plastic tongue and wheels that turn. $145-195

Stagecoach pin. Carved Catalin front and wheels that turn. Painted carved wood, brass trim. *Courtesy Lori Kizer.* $145-195

Painted carved wood stagecoach pin. Plastic tongue, brass trim, oilcloth awning, and wheels that turn. $95-145

Different type stagecoach pin. Front view of driver, and oxen with plastic horns, painted carved wood. $65-95

Down Mexico Way

Mexican man wearing sombrero pin. Painted carved wood. *Courtesy Lori Kizer*. $45-65

Painted carved wood guitar and sombreros pin, brass chain. $65-95

Painted red Catalin Mexican pot pin. Painted carved wood sombreros, brass trim. $200-300

Painted carved wood Mexican man pin. Carrying yellow plastic 'mescal jug' attached with jute, his arm swivels. $125-225

Painted carved wood Mexican man pin. Arm on swivel freely moves as wearer of pin walks, causing the man to appear to be playing the fiddle! $125-225

Painted machine stamped wood Mexican man (taking siesta) pin. Note child's tooth marks on sombrero. $15-30

Primitively carved guitar playing painted wood Mexican man pin. Arm swivels. $75-145

Colorful painted Catalin Mexican man pin. Painted carved wood sombrero. $300-500

Mexican leading burro pin. Painted carved wood, plastic bridle. $195-295

Pair of smokers pins. Machine-stamped painted wood. $45-65

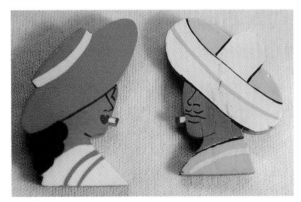

Military Emblems

World War II prop plane pin. Carved painted wood with propeller that turns. $95-145

Bullets and jeeps in World War II! Carved butterscotch Catalin bullet bar pin with suspended carved wood jeep, painted details. *Courtesy Lori Kizer*. $300-500. Rare.

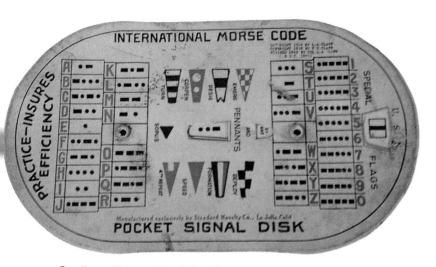

Cardboard International Flag Code Pocket Signal Disk from World War II. $20-40

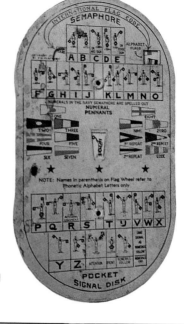

Reverse side of Signal Disk, dated 1942.

Carved wood Victory pin with clear lucite wings. *Courtesy Jean Bybee.* $65-125

Red lucite key, plastic V with inset rhinestones, World War II Victory Pin. $95-145. Blue leather (home kit) World War II bar pin with glued metal flag. $35-55

Right:
World War II soldier. A googly-eyes painted celluloid Army pin. *Courtesy Lori Kizer*. $65-95

Clear lucite anchor pin with carved wood USN. $65-125

Carved wood World War I sailor pin, painted with googly-eyes. *Courtesy Barbara Wood.* $65-95

Right:
Carved cedar wood World War II pin. U S A - Berlin, G I Shoes Over Germany. $45-65

Carved wood World War II airplane pin. U S Army. $45-65

Carved wood World War I
sailor pin with paint almost
gone. $35-55

Right:
Wood World War II bar pin. Carved and
painted pair of sailors on celluloid links.
$65-95

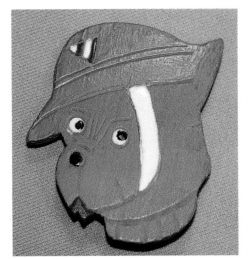

Carved wood World War I dog head pin with
helmet, painted details. $45-65

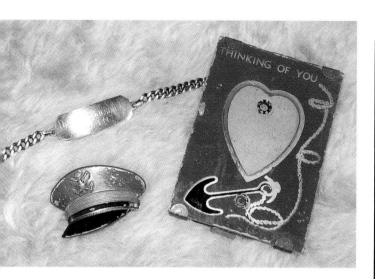

World War II items including small painted glass picture frame. $10-20. Painted metal officers hat pin. $20-40. Sterling silver identification bracelet worn by many soldiers during the war years. The I D bracelets were still popular well into the 1950s. $35-55

Non-wooden Lapel Pins

Lapel pin. Josephine Baker painted ceramic face, suede tie/ hat, wood trim, brass earrings. 1940s. $95-195

Lapel pin. Smoking monkey with painted ceramic face, felt hat, purple suede tie, wood cigarette. 1940s. $65-125

Lapel pin. Singing guitar-strumming Mexican man with painted ceramic body, large straw hat, woven fabric scarf, secured to wood base. 1940s. $75-150

Lapel pin. Fanciful donkey with painted ceramic body, lucite ears and tail. 1940s. $65-95

Lapel pin. Painted Egyptian type face with embroidered fabric/felt headpiece. Probably a home kit. 1940s. $45-65

Right:
Lapel pin. Showgirl with painted ceramic face, suede/leather headpiece, glass bead trim. Pin back is a small safety pin attached to suede. 1940s home kit (note lop-sided set of rhinestone earrings). A lot of jewelry was made by using home kits during this period, and ceramic clay was one of the favorite mediums. $20-40

Lapel pin. Painted sleepy-eyed white-spotted green ceramic giraffe. 1940s. $25-45

Below:
Handmade felt lapel pins, one a Yuma, Arizona souvenir, verify that felt was used for jewelry in the 1940s. Heavily embroidered felt jackets, the concept originating in Mexico, were very popular during that time, and these are still sought after today by vintage clothing lovers, the really nice ones commanding high prices. Lapel Pins $15-30

Lapel pin. Whimsical painted green ceramic pony with red saddle. 1940s. $25-45

Leather footballs and what looks to be a uniformed Russian soldier, with painted wood bead head, showcase handmade pins using leather, another 1940s wartime favorite. Still on original cards, made in USA. $25-45

Right:
A group of felt and leather lapel pins. Top, a home kit felt canoe and three Scotties. $10-20. Right, World War II stuffed leather bar pin with metal glued on flag. $35-55. Left, leather souvenir elephant bar pin. Hermann Park Zoo. 1940s. $15-30

Handmade leather World War II soldier bar pin. $15-30

Leather bird lapel pin. 5" tall, wood bead head. Probably home kit. 1940s. $45-65

Western hat/gloves leather lapel pin. Colorful 3.5" trimmed with brass and braid. 1940s. $45-65

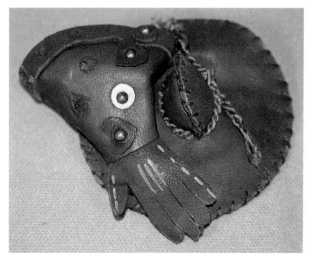

Leather boots/horseshoe/riding crop lapel pin. 4.5" trimmed with brass. 1940s. $45-65

Nuts were used extensively between 1940-45 in jewelry and figures. Here's a 5" cowboy with walnut body, pecan head, bean arms and legs, painted face, small plastic hat. $35-55

Close-up of walnut body. Sawn and hinged, when opened it reveals a tiny bride and groom. Perhaps a gift for a newly married couple from the southwest?

These molded plastic pins were very popular during the 1940s, and the western and Mexican themes were both favorites! In good shape, with their color retained and their pin back in working order, these pins can command a good price in today's market. $10-40

Necklaces

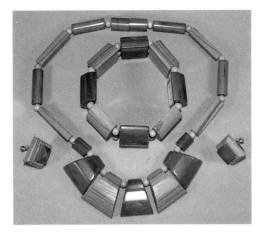

Necklace, bracelet, earrings set. Combination pale wood/green Catalin. *Courtesy Lori Kizer*. Set $75-150

Carved dark wood beads/ leaves bar pin and bracelet set. *Courtesy Lori Kizer*. $65-95

Intricate carved wood necklace, shown with green Catalin/wood button earrings and cedar wood circle earrings. *Courtesy Lori Kizer*. Necklace $65-95, Earrings $15-30

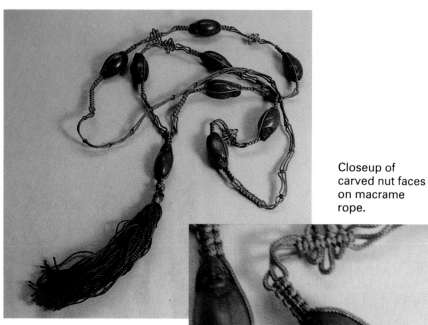

Closeup of carved nut faces on macrame rope.

Macrame tasseled flapper-style rope. Rayon cord worked with carved nuts. Exact age unknown. $20-40

Choker. Carved dark wood leaves and acorns on brass chain. $45-65

Right:
Choker. Painted wood heart pendant on celluloid chain. $20-40

Choker. Petrified wood strips on celluloid chain. $65-95

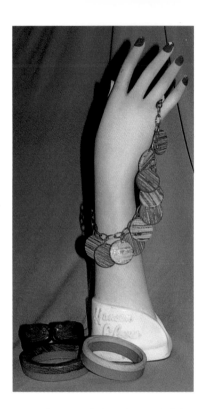

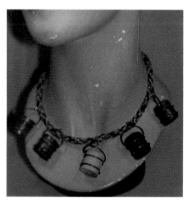

Choker. Stained carved wood buckets with brass trim on twisted rayon cord. $45-65

Choker. Painted wood disks on celluloid chain. Shown with two wood/plastic bangles and a wood/plastic combination hinged bracelet. Choker $45-65

Three piece choker set of wood and brass beads. $20-40

Choker. Painted carved wood sombreros on twisted cotton cord, matching earrings. $65-95

Choker. Real nuts on celluloid chain. $45-65

Choker. Carved wood circles with painted carved wood fish attached to leatherette chain. $65-95

WoodenNovelties

Address Markers

Farm gate address plaque. Painted and carved pine wood horse figure, 18.5" long. 1930s. *Courtesy Andrew Church Antiques*. $145-195

Right:
Primitive stained hand carved pine mail box. Six pieces of wood were used to fashion this box in 1915. Joel Leslie Boies was the author's grandfather, and this mailbox was used on his front porch from the time it was made until his death in 1952. $45-95

Advertising Souvenirs

Intricate carved wood canoe in original box, Honolulu Souvenir Canoes. 1940s. $25-45

Painted carved wood picture frame. Cowboy face with frame for picture insert at bottom. Souvenir of White Lake, North Carolina. 1940s. $25-45

Painted wood heart-shaped base tin dinner bell reads "Good bread . Good meat . Good gosh . Let's eat". Bell can be removed and has clapper. Texas souvenir. 1950s. $15-30

WHILE YOU WASH THE DISHES,
WHILE YOU WASH THE CLOTHES,
YOUR RINGS WILL BE SAFE,
HANGING HERE ON MY NOSE.
San Antonio, Texas

Kitchen window sill ring holder for the dishwashing housewife. Painted wood. San Antonio, Texas souvenir. 1950s. $5-15

Clarksdale, Mississippi souvenir calendar. Painted carved wood. 1940s. $15-30

Animal Figures

Mahogany running elk. Carved wood mantle decoration from the northwest area. 11" figure sanded and smoothed to perfection. 1930s. *Courtesy Andrew Church Antiques*. $65-125

Attentive dog on base carved from one piece pine. 3.5" tall with excellent detail. 1930s. *Courtesy Andrew Church Antiques*. $30-60

Above:
Painted carved wood donkey cigarette dispenser. Large novelty item. Loose cigarettes are inserted in donkey's backpack. Twist his ear, and guess where cigarette comes out? 1950s. *Courtesy Lori Kizer*. $15-35

Bar-b-que Markers

Carved wood meat gauge figures for bar-b-ques. Each figure rests on oversize toothpick, and can be inserted into a steak. Reads "If your guests are hard to please, Mark the hunks of meat with these". 1950s. $10-20

Triangular meat gauge corral with 12 painted wood figures for bar-b-ques. 1950s. $15-25

Belts

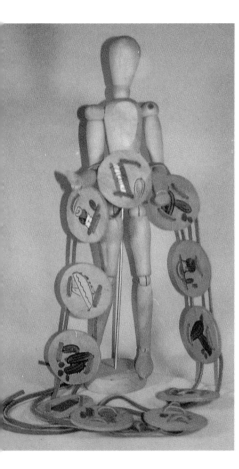

Painted carved wood Mexican belt. Disks held with rawhide strips. 1940s. $15-25. Displayed on jointed wood artist figure.

Close-up of painted wood belt disk. 1940s. $3-6

Painted wood disks Mexican belt with 3" colorful Mexican plates alternating with 2" sombreros, held with twisted rayon cord. 1940s. $15-25

111

Bookends

Buttons, Beads, Buckles & Charms

Painted wood and metal pair of bookends depicting older style school desks. Base/desk tops/books are carved wood. Note apple and ink well on desk top. 1950s. $15-35

Colorful wood buttons of painted Mexican plates and flower pots. 1950s. $3-6

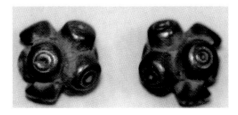

Carved stained wood three dimensional beads. $2-4

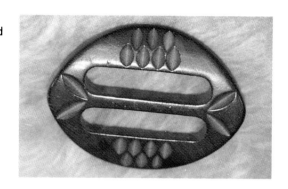

Right:
Carved wood ladies' buckle stamped Czech on back. 1930s. $4-8

Button, button, who's got the .... ? Four brown celluloid buttons decorated with wood strips secured by metal rings. Note color in two buttons has faded. 1920s. $6-12

COCONUT BUTTONS
MADE FROM FLORIDA COCONUTS

Carved by Natives

Buttons and buckles were the linchpin of many novelty companies during the 1930s and 40s. These coconut buttons and buckle from that period are still on card reading 'Carved by Natives'. $20-40

Carved wood laminate two color ladies' buckle and matching buttons. 1930s. $8-12

Colorfully painted carved wood charms made in Mexico. 1940s. $4-8

Carved wood charms/nuts. 1940s. $4-8

Christmas Ornaments

Unique Christmas tree ornaments made during the Depression from walnuts. $4-8

Painted carved wood Christmas tree ornaments including elephant, rocking horse, boy on shooting star, plane, horse, steamboat, man on the moon. Probably 1970s. $2-4

Dressing Items

Dark brown coconut shell child's purse. Painted face, satin cord handle, fabric lined, elastic hooks onto bead nose for closure. Hawaiian souvenir. $10-20

Perhaps because of all the beautiful woods available in Hawaii, that part of the world has always seemed to appreciate what could be done with wood, as evidenced in this beautiful wood compact with painted top. 1950s. *Courtesy Jean Bybee.* $45-65

Pale tan coconut shell purse with yarn top-knot and big-eyed painted face. In both these purses top of shell is sawn off, then hinged at back with yarn, fabric lined.

The inside of the compact indicates it was never used.

Called Pyro Art, Victorian ladies of leisure pursued this art form. This wood box is 32" long and only 5" wide. Standing on brass knob feet and satin lined, fanciful patterns of leaves, curliques, flowers, griffins, seashells and a ladies' face have been burned into the wood. *Courtesy Lori Kizer.* $65-145

Close-up of upraised lid and center compartment of Victorian wood box.

Buckarettes By Karoff. Western motif perfumes in cardboard box. Painted wood face/tops with fabric clothes and hats. $65-95

Large, heavy factice display of CIE perfume filled with colored alcohol. Top is cream painted wood and accounts for 9" of total 14" height. Exact age unknown. *Courtesy Lori Kizer*. $65-125

Painted carved wood ladies' wedgies from the Philippines. Full, front and side views shown. This or something similar still available to tourists. $20-40

Painted wood Dutch shoes, used by gardeners in Holland, and sold as souvenirs for many years in that country. $15-30

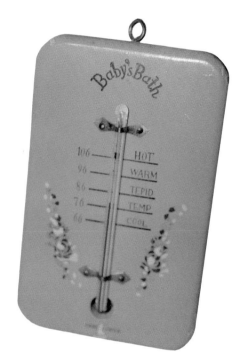

Painted wood baby's bath thermometer. Still works. 1930s. $10-20

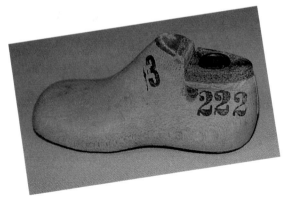

Wood shoe last for baby shoe. $8-12

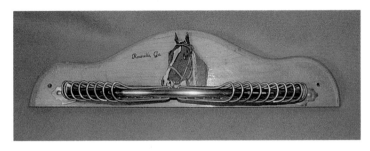

Glossy pine wood tie bar with raised horsehead. Metal bars swivel to hold men's ties. Rossville, Georgia souvenir. 1940s. $10-20

Close up of tie bar's raised horsehead.

Games

Wood poker chip holder of beautiful natural wood on swivel base with brass grip. New. $15-35

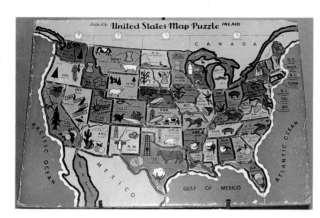

Colorful cardboard puzzle of the United States ... before Alaska and Hawaii became states. *Courtesy Jim Carlile/A. B. McGill Antique Emporium*. $15-30

Still in the gambling genre, a carved wood hand pin with suspended wood circles and red Catalin dice. 1940s. *Courtesy Lori Kizer*. $95-195

Five old wood gaming dice with Catalin dice and brass screw-back earrings. 1940s. $2-4, $10-20

Key Chains & Key Racks

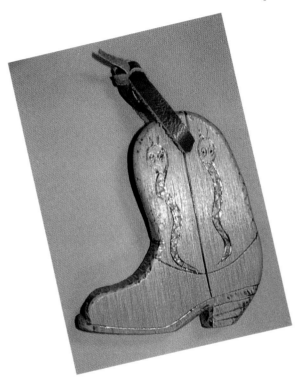

Carved wood boot key chain with burned in snake hi-lights, leather chain. $4-8

Painted handmade pine horsehead key rack with rope, brass trim. Reads "If a man has enough horse sense to treat his wife like a thoroughbred she will never become an old nag". 1930s. $25-45

Kitchen Items

Cholla cactus items have been available in southwestern states for many years at tourist stops. On the left, a small wagon night light of cholla wood with paper shade of Arizona desert scene. On right, painted chalk salt/pepper set in cholla wood base. Exact ages unknown. $10-30

Handmade pine egg crate with metal handle. 1940s. *Courtesy Jimmy's Antiques*. $20-40

Graceful 7" tall solid wood goblet with rawhide strip trim around stem. $6-15

Wood ice bucket with decal pheasant scene. Plastic insert, copper top and handle, wood knob on top. 1950s. $8-18

Left:
Machine made wood drink coaster. Painted scene of sexy girl leaning against lamp post. A Pick Me Up! 1950s. $3-9

Handmade (probably hobby kit) large matchbox holder for kitchen matches. Painted Mexican figure with guitar. 1940s. $10-20

Machine made wood hot pad holder with raised painted Mexican figure. San Antonio, Texas souvenir. 1950s. $6-18

Left:
Hawaiian monkey pod wood napkin holder. Carved and varnished, with likenesses probably still available in the Islands. $6-10

Right:
Left, bowler's wood place card holder with wood pin, black marble ball, slot for placecard. Right, table favor bar pin for the bowler. 1950s. $4-10

Below:
Machine made wood napkin rings with painted bluebonnets, the Texas State flower. $3-6

Right:
Carved wood cart holding nut hedgehog salt/pepper shakers on peg legs, with cork noses, painted eyes. Pueblo, Colorado souvenir. 1950s. $6-18

Two painted carved wood horse-drawn wagons carrying souvenir wood salt/pepper sets. *Courtesy Arlene Cassens*. 1950s. $25-45

Cedar wood clock shaped salt/pepper shakers. 1950s. $6-18

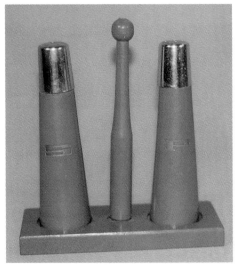

Machine made green painted wood salt/pepper set in small handled tray. 1970s. $4-12

Lovely light colored wood tray with chrome handle trim with painted map of the Hawaiian Island chain. 1950s souvenir. $8-18

Dark carved wood serving tray, 22 x 14, with glass insert. From Mexico. Exact age unknown. Can also be used as a wall hanging. *Courtesy Lori Kizer.* $15-30

129

SHOPPING REMINDER

- BACON
- BREAD
- BUTTER
- B.POWDER
- B.SODA
- BISCUITS
- CAKE
- CHEESE
- CLEANSER
- COFFEE
- CRACKERS
- CREAM
- DETERGENT
- EGGS
- FLOUR
- JAMS
- JUICES
- LEMONS
- MATCHES
- MEATS
- MARGARINE
- ORANGES
- ONIONS
- PEPPER
- POTATOES
- PEAS
- RICE
- SALT
- SOUPS
- SOAP
- SPICES
- STARCH
- SUGAR
- TEA
- TOOTHPASTE
- VINEGAR

Left:
Machine made wood shopping reminder for kitchen wall. Red pegs fit into holes to help a busy 1950s housewife keep up with her shopping needs. $15-30

Right:
An earlier wood shopping reminder with very few choices, perhaps because in the 1930s Depression there was little money to buy outright, and much of the food consumed was grown by the consumer. Note cracked edge, obliteration of apples on list, all pegs missing. Old age or child-related damage? $4-12

From Mexico a painted wood liqueur set. Bottle with matching tray, 6 small footed glasses. 1950s. *Courtesy Jimmy's Antiques.* $25-45

Black Americana liquor bottle stopper. Chrome over cork with painted wood face and red wood fez which hides a chrome pour spout. 1940s. $15-30

Rooster pencil holder. 9" tall totally worthless do-dad! Nevertheless, a clever take and pleasing to those with a sense of humor. Solid wood cone body with head attached by spring, it constantly moves. Painted eye, beak with red/green felt trim and a 12-pencil tail. Everybody needs one! 1950s. $15-35

Every home in the 1950s had an item made with wood popsicle sticks, usually by a child in Vacation Bible School! Here the wood sticks have been used to make frames to hold small chalk kitchen wall plaques of an apple and an ear of corn. $6-10

Popsicle stick church with over 75 sticks artfully cut, notched, glued to form the building, and steeple. 1950s. $6-10

132

Texas size rolling pin, carved from one piece of Texas cedar with natural knot-holes. 25" long. New. *Courtesy Jimmy's Antiques*. $35-50

Left:
Every American home saved trading stamps and many homes had a wood box such as this to keep them from being misplaced. 1950-60s. Trading stamps still available in some parts of the United States. $10-20

Wooden cannister set with Western cow branding decoration. 1950s. *Courtesy Ed Gage*. $45-65

Masks

Left:
Beaver Headdress Ornament with Sealion Bristles, 15" tall, handcrafted of thornwood, signed Philip Thorn (Canada). Exact age unknown. *Courtesy Jimmy's Antiques*. $85-150

Right:
A group of five old painted carved wood ceremonial masks from a collection sold in a San Angelo, Texas estate. All done using tree trunks, including this 10" red devil mask with goat horns. Note snakes carved up each side of face. 1930-40s. *All five masks Courtesy Jimmy's Antiques*. $175-350

Brightly painted tiger mask with open mouth, wicked teeth.

Medusa mask with coiled rope effect of snakes. Note wood carved snake heads at rope ends by chin.

Pig mask with painted eyes with glass coverings, boar tusks and stiff boar hair added, and painted pigskin ears.

Ladies painted face mask with eye holes for wearer cut out above painted eyes, trimmed with bamboo.

People

Wood/shell Hawaiian black American souvenir novelty figures. 1940s. $5-15

Left, black American wood bowling gift novelty in cellophane pack. Reads "Half S Bowler - For Making 50% of All Splits & Spares". 1940s. Right, wood figures in boat, paper palm tree black American souvenir thermometer novelty, either Hawaii or Florida. 1940s. $15-30

Another wood/shell black American thermometer souvenir with paper palm tree. 1940s. $15-30

Florida souvenir black American wood piece, pine cone body. 1940s. $15-30

Metal/shell Hawaiian black American souvenir novelty with painted cork head. 1940s. $15-30

Left:
Assorted bottlecap men.
1950s. $45-75

Closeup of well done black bottlecap
man. Wood body, head and base,
plastic hat and basket, felt and brass
trim. 1950s

Most bottlecap men were just that ... men ... but here's a gal with a leather bra! 1950s

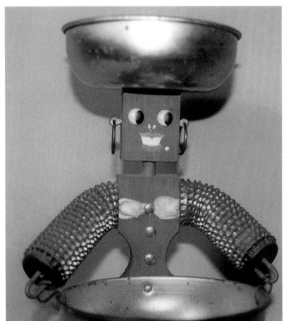

Closeup of bottlecap gal.

Handmade doll in the likeness of Carmen Miranda. Felt 9" tall body, rayon clothing, painted face, base and platform shoes of carved wood. Fabric fruit and headpiece. 1940s. $75-150. Shown with two carved wood/plastic pins and a wood 'valuables' box with brass and pewter trim.

Colorful tin noise maker with
Carmen Miranda look ... girl with
fruit-topped hat! 1940s. $15-30

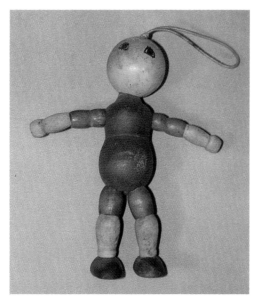

Machine made painted wood crib toy with
elastic top knot. This type figure very popular
now as a Christmas tree ornament. 1930s.
$25-45

Clothespin cowboy and cowgirl. Painted
wood figures have felt hats, silk neckties,
pipe cleaner arms, twine ropes. Girl has felt
vest and skirt, plus tiny pot metal gun in
plastic holster. 1940s. $35-55

Closeup shows painted features. Eye holes are lined inside with sheer fabric allowing light to easily shine through.

Unusual lamp/night light from Brazil measuring over 36" tall, set on driftwood base. Wood dowel body, rough burlap type clothing stuffed with straw. Brown raffia hair. Coconut head sawn at top, hinged on back with light behind eyes. 1960s. $35-55

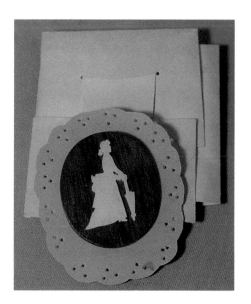

Known as Marlow Woodcuts, these were made of a very thin round wood base of three pieces glued together - dark-light-dark - with natural wood silhouette glued to round base. Pin back glued on, and wood piece attached to pierced construction paper, then put into its own cardboard folder. These originated in Americus, Kansas and are probably from the 1940s. $6-12

It is totally amazing that anything made from pipe cleaners would still be around after 50 years, but this pipe cleaner figure is a good example of 1940s pipe cleaner work. On a wood base with painted wood bead face, hat and baton, the plastic Cocktail Recipes holder on arm contains 6 tiny, but readable, cocktail recipes . $20-40

A drunk on a lamp-post? Perhaps this pipe cleaner figure was meant to convey that idea with his painted wood bead face, hat, and walking stick. 1940s. $20-40

Pipe cleaner ladies figure twirling
twine rope on wood base with plastic
bead painted face. 1940s. $10-20

Bow legged cowboy figure.
Pipe cleaner legs, ribbon
body, wood bead painted
face, plasteen rope. 1940s.
$10-20

Pipe cleaner pin, body made
entirely of twisted pipe cleaners.
1940s. $6-10

Group of three handmade figures made from nuts, paper, pipe
cleaners, pine cones, brass, twigs, wood beads and dried
beans. 1940s. $25-45

This turkey on a stick may have been a
table favor. Painted wood bead head, pine
cone body, felt and pipe cleaner trim.
1940s. $15-30

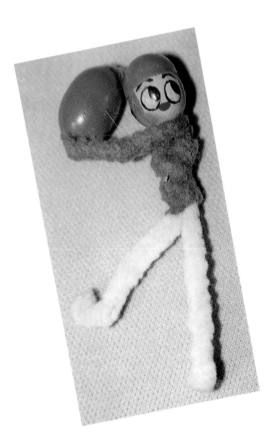

Pipe cleaner football player pin.
Painted wood bead head and
football 1940s. $15-30

Vegetable girl. 10" tall on wood base made of pipe
cleaners, flannel, and wire, with a stuffed nylon
head and painted face. 1950s. $20-40

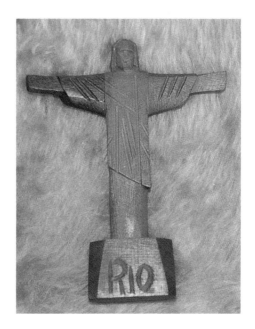

Three monkeys in a coconut tree. On a glass base, these pipe cleaner monkeys have celluloid heads, and reside in pipe cleaner trees with crepe paper trunks! 10" tall. 1950s. $65-95

Wood carved figure of Jesus from Rio. Souvenir from Brazil. Some form of this likeness probably still available. $6-10

Pictures

Two Mexican carved wood pictures with painted detailing and carved wooden frames.

Pair of painted wood pictures. Mexican boy and girl strumming guitars. 1950s. $10-20

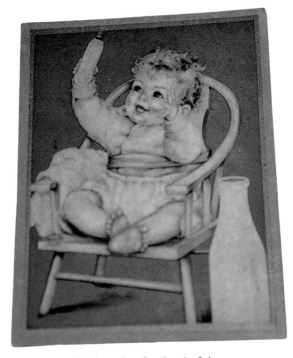

Darling small baby print. 3 x 4 colorful paper print laminated to wood back, 1930s. $6-12

A group of carved wood pictures, 1940-50s, all hunting scenes, perhaps high school 'shop art'. Left, 17 x 17 brown cedar shake carved bird hunter with dog in grassy field. Center, 5 x 7 carved oak dog and hunter, painted black and white. Right, 11 x 11 cedar shake carved and painted hunter with dog in colorful winter scene. *Courtesy Andrew Church Antiques.* $45-125

150

Solid wood picture with frame and scene all carved from one flat piece of a colorful painted Mexican scene, with rope hanger. Exact age unknown. $25-45

Cedar wood tacky plaques, too crude for most and widely used as gag gifts, this one a souvenir from Las Vegas. $5-15

Not quite so tacky, this little desk top homily from Boys Ranch in Amarillo, Texas is more truthful than most. $4-8

Family Dog House plaque. Whichever family member ends up in the dog house, his removable dog figure can be placed there until he redeems himself. 1950s. $15-30

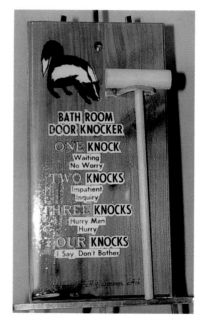

Hot Springs, Arkansas souvenir. This type souvenir can still be found in some tourist stops. $5-15

Postcard Mailers

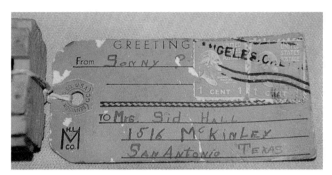

Yes, this postcard and attached orange crate (with three views shown) were mailed through the United States Post Office in the 1940s. This small wood crate, holding (wood bead) oranges, was sent from Los Angeles to San Antonio for 2 cents! Date didn't stamp properly, so can't be exactly dated. $15-30

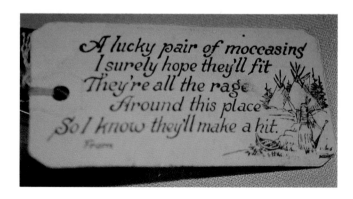

Another postcard mailer, these tiny 2.5" beaded suede moccasins were never mailed, but were meant for that purpose. A Southwestern souvenir. 1940s. $15-30

Very popular during the 1940s, here's another postcard mailer. An owl sent from New Mexico to Venus, Texas, but postmark not discernible. $15-30

This postcard mailer has a readable postmark - 9 Sep 45 - mailed by a Californian in Tijuana, Mexico to Temple, Texas with a small straw sombrero attached. $20-40

Date not readable on this mailed orange crate, but postage had risen to six cents, so it was mailed from Florida to Cincinnati, Ohio at a later date. Rather than wood beads, this orange crate contained cellophane-wrapped candy from the Sunbeam Novelty Company in Miami, some of which can still be seen in the little crate. $15-30

Toys

Child's toy wood horse with painted saddle and eye. $2-4

156

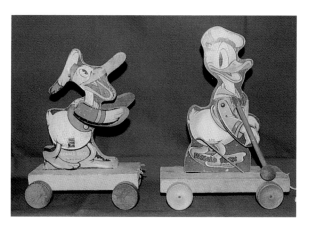

Two terrific Walt Disney pull toys. On the left, a Fisher-Price wood Donald Duck pull toy. Paper glued to wood base, arms stapled to rubber through wood slot at back neck, signed (C)W.D.Ent.1936. On the right, another Fisher-Price wood Donald Duck pull toy. Paper glued to wood base, right arm attached to metal plunger with stick. When pulled, toy makes noise. Signed (C) W.D.P. 1946. *Both Courtesy Tim Pierson*.

Painted wood doll furniture with straw seats from Mexico. $20-40

Handmade balsa wood doll house furniture with vinyl insert trim. $6-12

Weathervane

Whirligig

Eagle weathervane. Carved and painted wood, 26" long from bill to wingtip. 1940s. *Courtesy Andrew Church Antiques.* $400-600

Solid oak, rocket ship whirligig, a shape right out of Buck Rogers Saturday morning matinees. 23" long, 8" tall. 1930s. *Courtesy Andrew Church Antiques.* $800-1200

Bibliography

Books

Baker, Lillian. *Art Nouveau & Art Deco Jewelry*. Paducah, Kentucky: Collector Books, 1981.

_____. *50 Years Of Collectible Fashion Jewelry 1925-1975*. Paducah, Kentucky: Collector Books, 1986.

_____. *100 Years Of Collectible Jewelry*. Paducah, Kentucky: Collector Books, 1978.

_____. *Twentieth Century Fashionable Plastic Jewelry*. Paducah, Kentucky: Collector Books, 1992.

Battle, Dee & Lesser, Alayne. *The Best Of Bakelite and Other Plastic Jewelry*. Atglen, Pennsylvania: Schiffer Publishing Ltd., 1996.

Becker, Vivienne. *Rough Diamonds*. New York: Rizzoli Publishing International Publications, Inc., 1991.

Bowen, Hilary. *Woodturning Jewelry*. East Sussex, England: Guild of Master Craftsmen Publications Ltd., 1995.

Davis, Mary L. & Pack, Greta. *Mexican Jewelry*. Austin, Texas: University of Texas Press, 1963.

Dawes, Ginny R. & Davidov, Corinne. *The Bakelite Jewelry Book*. New York: Abbeville Press, 1988.

Dawes, Ginny R. & Davidov, Corinne. *Victorian Jewelry, Unexplored Treasures*. New York: Abbeville Press, 1991.

DiNoto, Andrea. *Art Plastic Designed for Living*. New York: Abbeville Press, 1984.

Grasso, Tony. *Bakelite Jewelry, A Collector's Guide*. New Jersey 08837: Quintet Publishing, Chartwell Books, 1996.

Husfloen, Kyle. *Black Americana Price Guide*. Dubuque, Iowa: Antique Trader Books, 1996.

Lynnlee, J. L. *All That Glitters*. West Chester, Pennsylvania: Schiffer Publications, 1986.

Mansperger, Dale E. & Pepper, Carson W. *Plastics, Problems & Processes.* Scranton, Pennsylvania: International Textbook Press, 1938.

Miller, Harrice S. *Costume Jewelry/Price Guide 2nd Edition.* New York: The Confident Collector Avon Books, 1994.

Moro, Ginger. *European Designer Jewelry.* Atglen, Pennsylvania: Schiffer Publishing Ltd, 1995.

Mulvagh, Jane. *Costume Jewelry in Vogue.* New York: Conde-Nast Thames & Hudson, Inc., 1988.

Romero, Christie. *Hidden Treasures, A Collector's Guide to Antique & Vintage Jewelry of the 19th & 20th Century.* Video. Sherman Oaks, California: Venture Entertainment Group, 1992.

Shields, Jody. *All That Glitters, The Glory of Costume Jewelry.* New York: Rizzoli International Publications, 1987.

Periodicals

Austin Home & Living. November-December 1997.

Breininger, Lester. "Tramp Art," Hanover, Pennsylvania: *Spinning Wheel*, March, 1969.

Comfort and Needlecraft. January 1942.

Elle Decor. December-January 1998.

Food & Wine. August 1996.

Harpers Bazaar. September 1997.

House Beautiful. September 1995.

Lauer, Keith."Convention 1995," *Vintage Fashion & Costume Jewelry Newsletter.* P O Box 265, Glen Oaks, New York 11004 Fall, 1995.

Life Magazine. May 13,1940.

McCall Needlework. Winter 1939-40, Summer 1945, Summer 1947, and Winter 1948-49.

Saturday Evening Post. August 10, 1940.

Tempesta, Lucille. "That's A Moure;" *Vintage Fashion & Costume Jewelry Newsletter.* P O Box 265, Glen Oaks, New York 11004: Summer, 1995.

Vogue. April 1995.

Yronwode, Catherine & Mullaney, Dean. *Collectible Plastics* (Newsletters). Guerneville, California: Society of Decorative Plastics: Vol. 1, No. 2, Dec 84-Jan 85; Vol. I, No. 3, Feb-Mar 85.